PEACE OF MIND THROUGH ESTATE PLANNING

A Guide for Georgia Residents - Protecting Yourself and Your Family

Sarah E. Siedentopf

PEACE OF MIND THROUGH ESTATE PLANNING
A Guide for Georgia Residents - Protecting Yourself and Your Family

© Sarah E. Siedentopf, 2019

ISBN: 978-0-578-65360-0

Table of Contents

Introduction

*I*f you are over the age of 18 and live in Georgia, this book is for you. It is pretty much as simple as that. Wait, you wanted more? This book is designed to introduce you to the topics you need to consider for your estate planning. As you familiarize yourself with the issues, you will notice that planning is just as important for a single person without children as it is for a parent. The main goals and motivating factors of your plan may be different, but the importance of taking care of yourself and your loved ones transcends age, gender, parental status, or relationship status.

At the end of this book, you will be familiar with many of the issues that may arise in your estate planning. You may choose to use this book to assist you with do-it-yourself estate planning. Once you read this book, you should feel more confident as you make choices and select options. Alternately, you may use this book to help you choose an attorney to do your estate plan. If you go that route, you will know the right questions to ask the attorney and understand the legal language ("legalese") that your attorney uses. You will also know whether your attorney is addressing all of the issues that are important to you.

What I hope to do is give you more knowledge and more confidence in your choices for estate planning. Sometimes we feel overwhelmed because we don't feel like we know which questions we should be asking. So, what does a Georgian need to know about estate planning?

A note about the importance of State law: The advice given in this book is based on Georgia law. If you don't live in Georgia, the rules and procedures in your state may be quite similar but can be completely different. If you are looking at estate planning outside of Georgia, I recommend you find a resource geared to your state law.

Protecting Your Children

*H*ow do I protect my children? While I argue that planning for yourself is just as important as planning for your children, this is typically the reason that parents of minor children come into my office.

We will look at choosing a guardian for your children, talking to your chosen guardian, and why designating a guardian for your children in your will is not enough. It is also important to have a standby guardian in case you are alive, but unable to care for your children. Other topics we will explore include the expanded options for powers of attorney in Georgia given to grandparents, what to do if you suddenly find yourself with physical custody of minor children but no legal guardianship, and designating conservators and trustees for taking care of money and property that belongs to your minor children. Finally, we will discuss things you should consider to make sure you leave enough money for your children.

Designating a Guardian in Your Will

One of the most important reasons to have a will is to name a guardian for your children. I have had conversations with potential clients that have gone something like this:

Me: "You should consider getting a will so that if something happened to you, your child would have a guardian."

Them: "But I have a sister, wouldn't my sister automatically get custody of my child?"

Me: "Do you have any other family, or does the child's other parent have any other family?"

Them: "Yes, my ex has a sister and parents."

Me: "Those other people have just as much chance of being your child's guardian as your sister does."

If you pass away and your child's other parent, their natural guardian, is alive and has not had parental rights terminated, then the other parent automatically becomes guardian. What if you're a single-parent and don't know where or who the child's other parent is? What if the father has never been legitimated and has no rights to the child? What if both parents are in an accident together? There are many possible reasons why the second parent might not be available to be a guardian for your child if something happened to you. The goal is not to dwell on the things that might happen, but to put your mind at rest by making sure that you have designated a guardian in your will.

It is a great first step to tell your friends and family who you would like to be guardian of your child if the worst were to happen. This isn't enough, however, because your verbally expressed wishes are not legally binding. The legal way to designate a guardian for your child is in your will. If you write it on a piece of paper, it is possible someone might find this piece of paper and show it to a judge— who might consider it when trying to decide who would make the best guardian for your child. But if you properly designate a guardian in your will, there should be no reason or need for a judge to have to determine who the best guardian is.

As you are considering guardians, you will also want to consider backup guardians. If for some reason your first choice of guardian is not available, there needs to be another option. Otherwise, the result may be the same as never having named anyone.

Choosing a Guardian

Choosing a guardian for your child is an important and serious task. It is important to begin by thinking about what duties the guardian will have. This will be the person who is making decisions about your child's education, making nutritional choices, and comforting and loving your child. You may want to consider someone who has a similar parenting philosophy to your own — someone whose judgment you trust. Other considerations when choosing a guardian include thinking about if it is important that a guardian has the same religious convictions you have or shares other values that are important to you.

Whether or not the potential guardian has children or wants children and how many children he or she has should also figure into your decision. A childless aunt or uncle might be thrilled to be named guardian, but if that person does not plan to have children of their own, this could also be an unwelcome burden. Conversely, if the potential guardian already has multiple children, how will your child fit in? Will the guardian have enough time and attention for an extra child or children?

As difficult as it is to think about, you may want to consider the socioeconomic class of the guardian you are considering. You likely imagine your child being raised in a similar environment to the one you would've provided. This could even encompass the location where the guardian lives. You may or may not want your children relocated outside the state, but the equation doesn't end there. You might be interested in someone who lives in a similar neighborhood or setting, whether that's rural or urban. You might be interested in someone who lives in the same school district as the one your child already attends.

Another important lifestyle issue is the age of the guardian. Grandparents may be excellent choices for guardians, but they will have limited energy and mobility issues that a younger guardian might not have. Choosing a guardian that is too young may result in being raised by someone not yet prepared to be a parent.

Pets are another important thing to consider. If it is important to you or your child to grow up with pets, a home that does not accommodate that may not be the best option. More acutely, if you have a child with severe allergies, you will have to be very sure of how a dog or cat owner would deal with the situation before deciding to potentially place your child in that household.

If your child has food allergies or special medical issues, you will want to think about whether the potential guardian either already has the knowledge or will be willing to learn how to manage these issues. Someone who does not "believe" in food allergies is not a good guardian for a child with peanut allergies. You should also make sure the potential guardian has the same medical stance on vaccination that you do. You should also consider personality and temperament when selecting a guardian. You want your child to have as much love and support as possible in a situation like losing a parent.

There are countless factors you may want to consider when naming a guardian. If you have multiple good options, consider yourself very lucky as you go through and rate the importance of the different qualities that each one brings. The thing that is most important to you might not be the thing that is most important to someone else, but that does not mean you should not trust your judgment. Make certain that you are true to yourself and your intuition rather than choosing an "obvious" choice that you have uncertainty or negative feelings about.

Also, keep in mind that a friend may end up being a better choice for a guardian than a family member. This can be hard because there is an unspoken assumption, or perhaps in some families a spoken assumption, that the child will stay in the family. However, if a friend will give your child the upbringing you desire, and family will ignore your desires and raise your child differently than you would want, you should not be shy about choosing the very best guardian for your child.

In a best-case scenario, both parents would agree on

guardians and name the same guardians for their children. If the two of you need help considering and discussing and agreeing upon guardians, it may be helpful to consult with a professional such as an estate planning attorney or a counselor.

Deciding Between Naming an Individual or a Couple

Once you've decided on a guardian, if that guardian is part of a couple, you will need to decide whether to name the individual or the couple as guardians. For example, if you name your brother and his wife as guardians, would you still want your sister-in-law to be the guardian if your brother were no longer living? Perhaps you have friends that together would make wonderful parents, but if they divorced, you might prefer someone else to be the guardian. Depending on how you word your document, you can choose an individual with no restrictions; a couple jointly as co-guardians, so that either member of the couple can continue as a guardian without the other; or an individual only if certain circumstances, such as remaining married to a certain person, are present.

Talking with Your Designated Guardian

Now that you have chosen a guardian, you need to formally ask the person if he or she is willing. Being named guardian might be a big honor but it also is a huge responsibility. Your nominee may need time to think over the possibility. It could be easy to be offended in this situation, but you want someone who is willing to think about what the task would actually require and commit to it thoughtfully. Being named as guardian in someone's will does not legally require you to accept the position, so you do want to know ahead of time that this individual or couple would be willing to act on your child's behalf.

You should set aside time to have a conversation with the potential guardian that isn't rushed. You might go out to dinner or sit down with a cup of coffee to have the conversation in as relaxed a setting as possible. Be prepared to answer questions the proposed guardian may have. Assuming that the guardian is willing, talk about anything that is especially important to you about how your child is raised. It is also a good idea to have some written instructions, but this is your chance to make sure they understand what you want for your child and are willing to be a part of that.

Standby Guardian

Congratulations, you've named a guardian for your children in your will. So we're good now, right? Actually, no. There are multiple kinds of guardians; you may want to consider naming a standby guardian as well.

What is a Standby Guardian?

What is a standby guardian, and how does it differ from the guardian you named in your will? An important thing to remember about your will is that it only takes effect when you are deceased. If you are alive and for some reason cannot care for your children, your will cannot help you. Someone could use your will as evidence of who you would like your child's guardian to be in a court hearing. But is a court hearing really what you want?

To avoid this, you want to name a guardian for your children and have it take effect immediately should you be in the hospital or otherwise incapacitated. In Georgia, this is called a standby guardian. If something happens to you or prevents you from caring for your child, the standby guardian has the legal authority to care for your child, enroll your child in school, take your child to the doctor, and do all the things you would want done for your child.

If you don't have a standby guardian and find yourself in the hospital unable to communicate, your child may be placed in the foster care system while the state figures out who should have custody. This outcome would be unnecessarily traumatizing to an already scared and vulnerable child.

Giving Good Instructions

You can prevent unfavorable or delayed outcomes for your children by legally naming a standby guardian and making sure that if something happens to you, people know who to call. If you don't pick your child up from school, the school should know who to call. Babysitters should know who to call if you don't come home. Daycare should know who to call. What you do not want is for the school, babysitter, or daycare to have no other option than to turn your child over to the Division of Family and Children Services (DFACS).

In addition to formally letting the school and daycare know who to contact in case of an emergency when they cannot reach you, there should be very clear instructions for anyone in your home. Having the name and phone number of your standby guardian on the refrigerator as part of a list of who to call in an emergency is a good place to start. Consider including a short sentence explaining when to call your standby guardian. Then, if an emergency occurs, your child would be safe with a trusted friend or family member, which is what you really want.

Grandparent Power of Attorney

Another special kind of guardianship is the grandparent power of attorney. There is a special law in Georgia that applies only to grandparents and allows parents to give a power of attorney to grandparents in case of hardship.

The term "hardship" is defined by the law, but the definition is broad and covers pretty much everything you might imagine. Much like with the standby guardian, the hardship could be the parent's inability to care for the child due to physical or mental illness. It also covers loss of the other parent or loss of a place to live, as well as several other contingencies.

The grandparent power of attorney can continue as long as the child is a minor, although it can be revoked by the parent or terminated by the court. Both parents are required to sign the grandparent power of attorney, except in a few exceptional circumstances, such as when a parent's parental rights have been terminated.

This power of attorney allows the grandparent to act as the parent would act. It allows them to enroll the child in school, get school records, take the child to the doctor, access medical records, and many other things.

The grandparent power of attorney could provide a way to make sure that your children are taken care of during a hardship event or, as a grandparent, could offer you an alternative to making sure that your grandchildren are safe.

Petition for Temporary Guardianship

Maybe as you are thinking that it's all well and good to have these pre-planning options, but you are past that and don't know what to do. You have found yourself with custody of a minor child and no legal authority over the child. First of all, thank you for being there for a child who needs you.

The good news is that in Georgia, temporary guardianship is an option. Any adult who has physical custody of a minor can petition the court for temporary guardianship of that child. There are a few exceptions, such as a requirement that the adult not also be a ward (have their own guardian) and not have a conflict of interest in taking care of the child. However, after a hearing, the court can waive a dispute if the guardian is still in the best interest of the child. You don't need to have any particular relationship to the child, so this works for an aunt, a grandfather, a best friend, or a neighbor. If you are taking care of a child for a lengthy or undetermined period, you may need to petition for temporary guardianship.

What to Do if You Have Custody of a Child

How does one petition for temporary guardianship? The Probate Court is the court that has jurisdiction over temporary guardianship in Georgia. You will need to file a petition with the Probate Court for the county that you and the child are living in. If you live out of state, as perhaps an extended relative might, the correct Probate Court is the Probate Court for the county the child is living in. Keep in mind, that while you don't need to live in Georgia to petition for temporary guardianship, you do need to have the child in your physical custody. Your visit to the state can be temporary, but you cannot petition for a child who is not presently living with you.

If there is a parent or parents available, they will need to be notified and approve of the guardianship. If a parent does not have legal custody of the child, then the parent will need to be notified. But the court will have a hearing and may approve the guardianship even with the objection of the parent. Notification is still required even if you don't know the address of the parent, which strangely enough, includes unknown fathers. For those without a known address, this notification is accomplished by publishing a notice in the newspaper. Each county has its own special paper called a "legal organ." Even though this doesn't necessarily result in the parent knowing about the temporary guardianship, it is still a legal requirement for the judge to move forward.

If the requirements have been met, the Probate Judge will have a hearing and decide if the guardianship is in the child's best interest. Then the judge will issue an order appointing a temporary guardian. This temporary guardian has all of the rights of a parent.

It is worth noting, however, that a temporary guardianship does not relieve the parent of his or her legal duty to support the child.

Conservator or Trustee?

Once you've thought about who should have physical custody of your child, you should start thinking about who should be in charge of assets that belong to your minor child. A guardian has control of a person, but a conservator or trustee is in charge of the money. A conservator would need to be appointed over your child's finances if you passed away without leaving things in a trust for your minor child. If you leave your money in a trust, you would be appointing a trustee to do the same thing. Because the roles of conservators and trustees are so similar, I will deal with them here together.

Choosing a Trustee

Many times parents will want the same person or persons to handle their child's finances that they picked to be the guardian. There is nothing wrong with this approach if you trust the guardian implicitly, and you must if you are entrusting that person with your child.

However, it is not always true that the best person to raise your child is also the best person for handling money. The skills necessary to be a good guardian, and the skills required to be a good trustee are not the same. Providing a safe, loving home for a child does not require knowing how to balance a checkbook. Having fiduciary responsibility (we will discuss fiduciaries later) for someone else's assets does require good financial skills.

Should the Trustee be the Same Person as the Guardian?

In addition to considering who in your life is best at managing money, you may also want to consider whether having a second individual or individuals overseeing your child is a desirable thing. The trustee is the one who will pay your child's bills, so the guardian will need to let the trustee know what expenses are incurred. This gives you a checks and balances system so that the money you have saved for your child does not go somewhere else. Even for people with the best possible motives, it can be easy to convince yourself that an expense that really ought to be borne by someone else is in a child's best interest. Having different people with different interests overseeing childcare and a child's finances makes misappropriating funds harder.

Ultimately, your choice will depend greatly upon who is in your life. Sometimes there are not multiple good choices, and the best option is to combine the roles of guardian and trustee. Sometimes, because you trust a person so thoroughly, it may be decided that the ease of having one person in charge of both child and money outweighs any desire for a second person to oversee things. But it is well worth considering your situation rather than giving a knee-jerk answer.

Considering Family Circumstances in Special Provisions for Your Trust

Another aspect to consider when thinking about what would happen to your child if you were no longer there are the financial circumstances in which they would be raised with the guardian you have chosen. Often you will find it desirable, if the guardian has children of his or her own, to have your child raised similarly to the guardian's children. This makes things easier on the guardian and easier on your child because it reduces feelings of difference and jealousy.

So what do you do if you know your sister is the best possible guardian for your child and that it is imperative to you that your child attends a private school, but your sister can only afford to send her children to public school? What about if you know that your chosen guardian lives in a small house and that it will be a financial burden to acquire a home with living space for your child? What if it is important to you that your child travel while young?

This is a specific area and must be tailored around your values, financial circumstances, and the guardian's circumstances. Generally speaking, the money you leave to your child in trust cannot be used to expand the guardian's house. It cannot be used to provide benefits for the guardian's family. It is, however, possible to put special provisions in a trust that allow for money to be spent on certain things you have approved ahead of time that would not otherwise be appropriate.

You could place a provision in your trust giving a special allowance to compensate the guardian for a specified amount or percentage of a change in a living environment that was due to adding extra children—your children. You could, for example, add a provision allowing money from your trust to be used to defray the cost of private school for the guardian's children if you decided it was in your child's best interest to have them all attend school together. You could give financial help for travel to the guardian's family, with whatever stipulations and limitations you desire.

Talking to Your Trustee

Once again, it is essential to have a conversation with your trustee nomination. This is a serious responsibility, and you want to be sure that you have chosen someone willing to undertake the duty.

You might take this opportunity to discuss your financial values with your trustee. You might also find that you and the child's other parent will need to dig deeper into your own financial values as you discuss what directives to give to your trustee. Let the trustee know if you would want your child to have an iPhone, what type of car you would buy for your child if you were around, and what type of education you would be planning to finance. While these conversations may seem morbid, they will assure you that if you are not around, the person in charge of your child's money will know how to spend it the way you would have spent it.

Leaving Enough Money

Another difficult topic to think about and discuss is leaving enough money for your children and/ or your spouse. The reality is that most of us don't have enough money in our bank accounts to take care of our families if the primary breadwinner disappears. The only way to combat this is to plan.

Planning ahead requires taking a realistic look at your finances and figuring out how to do some saving. Thankfully, saving is not the only possible option for leaving money for your children.

Life Insurance

If you have young children or a spouse who makes less than you do, it is important to consider life insurance. You may need to talk to more than one agent before you find one that you're comfortable with.

Sometimes there may be some life insurance, even subsidized life insurance, available at your place of employment. This may be the first place to look when you're thinking about life insurance.

There are also many different types of private policies, most of which require some sort of physical exam. Because of this, it is worth considering getting life insurance while you are young and healthy and feel that you could never need it. If you have a sudden medical issue, you might find yourself unable to get life insurance or to pay a significantly increased rate.

How much life insurance do you need? This varies from person to person and situation to situation. You're going to want to consider how many children you have, what kind of costs are associated with raising them, and how much longer those costs will last. You might want to consider leaving enough money for your spouse or children to pay off the house so they won't need to move and uproot themselves. You will want to leave enough money, if possible, for your children to go to college.

You also need to consider your spouse. Retirement may seem like a long time away for some, but if your retirement plans are based on two people working, or possibly only based on you working while your spouse stayed home, your spouse could be in a precarious situation without your income.

In an ideal world, you would leave enough life insurance to cover the rest of your projected lifetime earnings. This means that your family would not be any worse off financially without you.

Most of us can't afford enough life insurance to put our families in the ideal world situation. That doesn't mean that this step can be skipped. Serious consideration should be given to having adequate life insurance.

College Savings Plans

Another vehicle many people use to finance their children's futures is a college savings plan. Commonly called a 529 plan, college savings plans in Georgia receive a state tax deduction or credit. This can help defray the cost of saving for college.

Signing up for one is relatively straightforward, and automatic deductions can be taken from your paycheck. The automatic deduction can be a relatively painless way of saving. With the tax deductions and the current student loan crisis, many people are trying hard to finance these plans for their children.

That said, if your choice is to save for your retirement or your child's college tuition, and you cannot contribute to both, is often considered wiser to save for your retirement. Your child will have much longer to save to pay off college than you have to save for your retirement.

One of the other problems with college savings plans is that not all children go to college. What happens to the money if the beneficiary doesn't go to college? The money in the account can be used for any higher education, which would include vocational and trade schools as well as two-year programs at colleges. Additionally, the recipient of the funds can be changed, so if one of your children is not enrolling in any higher education and you have a second child, you can use the money for the second child. You could even use the money to send yourself back to school or another family member such as an aunt, uncle, or grandparent.

But what happens if no one is going to use this money for higher education? This is the catch. You will pay income tax and a penalty on the earnings. It is a steep downside and should be considered when deciding the best vehicle for providing for your children.

Saving

And then there is saving. Good old-fashioned saving. You will want to talk to a financial advisor about the best places for you to invest your savings — whether it's an emergency fund in a bank, an IRA or other retirement accounts, or general investments. But there's no way around the necessity for saving.

You don't need me to tell you, that the earlier you start saving, the more your money will compound and the greater the result, even with smaller contributions. While some people are genuinely not in a position to put away any savings, most of us can make lifestyle decisions that allow us to do so. Even small monthly savings will grow and can be used as a starting place for raising your savings as your income goes up.

When you think about your priorities and the reason you are saving—retirement, children, vacations, etc. — it becomes slightly less painful to lose the availability of the income now. It may no ever be easy, but it is always worthwhile.

Pets

For many of us, pets are like family, and making sure they are protected in the event of an emergency is a high priority. This requires some thought and planning because there is a higher likelihood that your pet would be home alone in a locked house when something happened than that your child would be left alone before they were old enough to call someone if they needed help.

In addition to the question of how to provide for your pet after your death, which will be discussed below, you should come up with a thoughtful plan for the immediate care of your pet in the event of an emergency. This might take the form of a card kept in your wallet next to your photo ID, which states that you have pets at home and gives instructions on who to call to care for them. It might also be that the emergency contacts in your phone have specific instructions on caring for your pets in the event of an emergency. However you want to handle the issue, make sure that someone will be coming to your pet's assistance.

Pets in Your Will

A popular choice when providing for pets is to put a provision in your will stating that the person who takes your pet gets a certain amount of money as a "thank you." The benefit of this is that it is relatively easy and straight forward and may help someone who loves your pet but is not financially secure be able to give your pet a loving home. The downside of this is that the money is a gift. This means that the person can take the money and drop your pet off at an animal shelter the next day and still be legally entitled to keep the money.

The people we choose to take care of our pets generally have personal emotional attachments to our pets and would not let them come to harm. So, leaving some money in your will is a nice gesture and unlikely to be abused. However, if you are leaving your pet to someone who loves you but does not have a relationship with your pet, you may want to explore other options.

Pet Trusts

Pet trusts allow you to set aside money specifically for the care of your pet in exactly the way you would put money in trust for a child. This will enable you to designate an individual to care for your pet, as well as someone to manage money for your pet. The finances are inextricably attached to the actual care of the pet, and the trustee cannot give money to someone who has given your pet away.

Pet trusts take a little more work to set up on the front end and have more administrative work than a one-time gift in your will. But they do make sure that the money actually goes to taking care of your pet and providing it a good home and not to beer and pizza for someone who is leaving your pet outside in the cold or has already given it away to someone else.

Protecting Your Assets

*N*ow that we've discussed protecting your children and pets, we will talk about protecting your assets. Even though we are discussing this as if it is about protecting your assets, it is essential to remember that this is really about protecting your family. Those dollars in the bank will not be sad if you are gone and do not need protection. On the other hand, your family needs ease of access to those funds and needs those funds to be conserved as much as possible.

Will

A will is one of the primary documents for protecting your assets. A will distributes your assets to exactly where you want them to go. It can also leave instructions about paying off debts or mortgages, your funeral arrangements, and can include a trust for minor beneficiaries or those with creditor problems.

What happens if you die without a will? Each state has its own laws about this. The rules of "intestate succession" in Georgia as of this writing are as follows:

1. If a single person passes away with no children, that person's parents will inherit from them. If the parents are no longer alive, siblings will inherit. If there are no siblings, the next in line are grandparents, and then aunts and uncles, and then cousins. The law reaches farther and farther in an attempt to find some relative. If no relative is found, the state gets it. This is called in escheat to the state.

2. If a married person passes away with no children, the spouse gets everything.

3. If a single person passes away, leaving children, the children get everything.

4. If a married person passes away, leaving children, the inheritance is split. The spouse can never get less than one third. If there is a spouse and one child, each gets half. If there is a spouse and two children, each gets one third. If there is a spouse and three children, the spouse gets a third, and the three children split the two thirds that are left.

Item number four is the tricky one. Most parents don't envision their children getting assets until their spouse has also passed away. In an unfortunate situation where a spouse dies, leaving the other spouse a one-year-old child, nobody wants the surviving parent and the one-year-old child to split things equally. What we expect is that the surviving parent will have all of the assets and will use them for the benefit of both the surviving parent and the child. Then when the surviving parent also passes away, the child will receive the assets.

If you don't have a will, and you have minor children, not only will there not be a testamentary guardian appointed, but dividing the assets can also be very difficult. It is not technically illegal to have a minor child on the deed of real property, but it can cause problems because you're going to have to jump through a lot of hoops if you need to transfer that property before the child turns 18. Also, if you have a situation where each spouse owns half of the house without the right of survivorship, and you leave several children, you can end up with a situation where the spouse owns one half of the property that was already in his or her name plus a third of the other half of the property. Then the children will own the other two-thirds of one half of the property. This can get very complicated and cause unnecessary confusion for your family.

Even in situations where you don't have many assets, leaving a will is kind to your family. Probate is more straightforward with a will then without a will. You are doing a good deed by leaving a will.

Duties of An Executor or Personal Administrator

One of the big choices you will make concerning your will is who to appoint as executor. What does this mean? What will your executor have to do? The basic idea is that this person is responsible to the court and to the other beneficiaries for opening up a probate estate, complying with the laws and regulations, paying the debts of the estate, and dividing the assets properly.

In practice, this will involve filing a petition to probate the will with the correct Probate Court. After that, the executor must "Marshall" the assets of the estate. This means finding out where everything is and gathering it together. This can involve going through paperwork left in file cabinets or offices, finding out where bank accounts are, finding out if there is a safe deposit box, finding the car title, finding the deed to the house, and maybe even finding addresses and locations for beneficiaries whose locations are unknown. The executor is responsible for posting a notice in the correct newspaper notifying creditors of the estate that they have three months to put in a notice of their claim. The executor will open a special estate bank account and put all of the funds from all other bank accounts into this account and use this account to pay bills. The executor will turn off Comcast and pay the final bill. The executor will notify the lawn care company that their services are no longer required or will let them know to keep the lawn looking pristine because the house is about to be sold. The executor will follow the terms of the will in selling the home or signing a deed to the correct beneficiary. After the executor has paid all of the bills, waited the proper amount of time, distributed assets to the right people, and received signed acknowledgments from those people, the executor can close the estate.

It can be difficult and overwhelming, particularly if there is unpleasantness within the family. Being executor can sometimes be described as a very thankless task. However, it is necessary and important.

Choosing an Executor

It is essential to choose the correct person for your executor and backup executor. It is tempting to think of this position as an honor, and in some sense, it is because it is a position of such high trust, but in reality, this is a demanding and challenging job. The executor should be chosen with thought as to who will do the best job and have the easiest time doing the job, not with as much emphasis on who might be honored by having the position.

An aging parent might not be the best choice for an executor because of mobility or cognitive complications. Just because you know that parent would feel a connection to you while performing this duty, does not mean that you should put it on them. However, advanced age does not prevent someone from doing an excellent job as an executor. Financial acumen and knowledge about the way the world works can be the stock in trade of those who have seen a greater number of years. This skill and knowledge make the process much easier. Attorneys can be hired, CPAs can be hired, and other family members can help.

The default choice for the majority of couples is that the other member of the couple is the first choice for an executor. This is often a great decision but should not be the only choice. It is always possible that both people will be in the same accident, but it is also possible that an otherwise capable and responsible adult may be to overcome by grief to want to be the executor or do a good job as executor. There should be second and third options, ideally, people who both parties are comfortable with so that if the surviving member of the couple can't or doesn't want to be in charge of the process of wrapping up the estate, they don't have to.

You will want to choose someone responsible, someone who can listen to advice, someone who has some knowledge of financial affairs, and someone who knows what they don't know. If you have an attorney or financial professional in your family, that person may seem like an obvious choice for an executor. But it isn't important that the person knows what they need to do. What is important is that the person is interested in doing a good job and knows enough to find help.

Leaving Instructions

In addition to instructions you leave in the will, you can place a paragraph in your will requesting that the executor honor the wishes you've written down in a letter. This letter doesn't have to be in existence at the time that the will is written, so you can change it and add to it over time.

Most of the time, this is used for instructions about specific people who should receive specific items of personal property. It might also relate to instructions for pets or instructions related to funeral details.

The beauty of the instructional letter is that it does not need to be as formal as your will. The downside of it is that it is not legally enforceable in the same way that your will is. It is up to the goodwill of the executor to follow the wishes in your letter. While this often works for personal property items, it would not be appropriate for gifts of money or expensive items, because of the risk of disagreement with other beneficiaries of the will.

You should also be careful not to write anything in your letter that conflicts with any actual terms in your will. An example of that might be putting in your will that a debt needed to be repaid and how that debt impacts the beneficiary's portion of the assets, and then leaving a separate note describing how the transaction should be calculated, which does not agree with the terms in the will. This always leads to disagreement and possibly lawsuits.

If you choose to leave instructions separately from your will, make sure that those instructions are found at the same time as your will. I suggest storing them together.

Per Capita vs. Per Stirpes

A confusing lawyer term that you may see in wills is that something should be divided per stirpes. Alternately, sometimes you will see that something should be divided per capita. What is the difference? How does it affect what happens?

The term per stirpes generally means by representation and per capita means by head. Initially, per capita sounds like the correct designation, because it sounds as if you are including everyone. What it means is that you include everyone currently alive in your classification. If you had three children and you divided assets per capita between them, if one of the children predeceased you, the other two children split the assets 50/50 and any grandchildren from the deceased child get nothing. This isn't necessarily wrong, but it is often not what you want to happen. In the same situation, if you were to divide something per stirpes, each of your two living children would receive one third, and the grandchildren from the deceased child would split that child's third between them.

The difference in these two terms, which sound similar and superfluous, could easily result in a significant amount of pain to your family. It could also result in not leaving your grandchildren anything when your actual intent was that they should receive something through your child, their parent.

If you see a word that you don't understand, make sure to look it up. Even small phrases can make a significant difference in what happens when your assets are divided.

Trust Inside Your Will for Minor Children

In a few pages, we will discuss standalone trusts or "inter vivos" trusts. But did you know that your will can contain a trust? This is a very important thing for parents of minor children to be aware of and take advantage of.

The beauty of having a trust inside your will is that you don't have to do anything to maintain it during your lifetime and changing it or revoking it is as easy as tearing up your will. There is no question of having a tax identification number for the trust inside your will or of needing to transfer property deeds into it. What it does is set up a trustee who will be in charge of any assets left to a minor child. This can also be used for assets left to needy beneficiaries, who need someone else to manage their funds.

Just like a regular trust, you can set all of the terms. You can decide at what age someone gets money and potentially divided it up into multiple sums at different ages. You can give direction to the trustee as to what it should be spent on. The list goes on and on because trusts can be very specific in their instructions.

Having a trust inside your will prevents anyone from having to go to court to set up someone to manage a minor's assets. It also prevents the court from appointing someone you wouldn't want to have been appointed.

Trusts are long and confusing and filled with legalese, so it can be tempting to ignore them in favor of clear and direct language. But often there is an actual benefit even if having a trust in your will results in an 18 page will instead of a five-page will. Parents of minor children should strongly consider adding one to their estate plan.

When to tell others about the contents of your will

An additional thing to consider and discuss with your partner if you have one, is whether to let people know ahead of time what they will be receiving in your will. There are various aspects of this to consider, and no one solution is right for every situation.

One aspect to keep in mind is that you might want to change your will. Sometimes this might have to do with conflict in a family, but it could be a much more benign reason. One of your two children might end up doing a significant amount of unpaid work that you would've otherwise had to pay a caregiver for. You might decide that instead of paying that child upfront, you would leave more to the caregiver in your will. You might make a will when you have two children and split things 50/50 between them but realize when you have grandchildren that you want a different distribution that specifically benefits the grandchildren in addition to benefiting the parents. Changing these things is as easy going to an attorney to create a new will and tearing up the old one. However if you have told your children that they are getting 50% of your assets and you have suddenly changed your mind, you have upset their expectations, and there may be a significant emotional backlash when you tell the children that you've changed your mind.

Conversely, in a situation where you are leaving more to one child than the other because one child has done significant caregiving activities, it might be beneficial to explain to the other child why you have done this. Knowing the reasoning behind your plan may keep the child who is getting less from thinking it is because the other child was your favorite. Telling people ahead of time can also prevent unwelcome surprises after your death and sometimes preserve family harmony.

The issue becomes especially charged if you are dealing with a second marriage and children from the first marriage. It is vital to consider your children's relationship with your spouse when making this calculation, but letting them know what to expect before the event may be a good idea. Alternately, it may lead to unpleasantness, or even charges that you cannot deal with your affairs and you need a guardian, so consider carefully before speaking.

Where to Keep Your Will

Now that you have a will, where should you keep it? There are various things to consider, such as security versus accessibility. Will people be able to find it when you're gone?

One option is to keep it with your important papers. You might do this in a filing cabinet or a fireproof lockbox. Fireproof has distinct advantages. Also, the idea of something secure such as a lockbox is attractive. If it's in a filing cabinet, you want to have it clearly marked in a reasonable organizational structure such as an alphabetical system.

Another option is to put it in your safe deposit box at the bank. This has less accessibility for you, but it is extremely safe. It is also a place that people know to look for wills. However, you also have to consider whether your executor will know what bank you have a safe deposit at or even that you have a safe deposit box.

A third option in Georgia is to file your will with the Probate Court in your county. This also has the advantage of being very safe, but it has the disadvantage that very few people will think to look for it here. Additionally, if you move at any time before your death, it may not be entirely clear where your will is. Also, if you want to change your will, getting it back from the bank or getting it out of your filing cabinet is significantly easier than going over to the courthouse and retrieving your will. I don't generally recommend this option because the court won't do anything with your will and your survivors probably won't know to look for it there.

Like almost everything else, this is an individual choice, and as long as your executor knows where to find your will, there are no wrong options.

What If I Lose the Original?

But what happens when you didn't store it properly, and you can't find it now? Maybe you have moved and somehow never found it while you are opening boxes. Maybe you've done a lot of reorganization and getting rid of things, and simply can't find it afterward.

If you are in a position to sign a new will, then you should do so. Courts significantly prefer original wills with ink signatures because the legal presumption, if you can't find an original will, is that there wasn't one or that it was destroyed. Destroying the will revokes it. Don't panic, but do sign a new original.

If we're past that point, for some reason, such as incapacity to sign a new will or the fact that the person has already passed away, also don't panic. The presumption that the will that cannot be found was destroyed and thus revoked is what's called a "rebuttable presumption." This means that while the court starts by assuming it is true and you can give evidence contradicting it and the court will change its mind if appropriate.

If you are trying to probate a copy of a will, you will have to explain to the court why the original was lost. This requires giving enough evidence for the court to believe that the original was inadvertently lost rather than destroyed and revoked. Although this is an extra hoop to jump through, is a fairly regular occurrence and courts are familiar with it.

How Can Someone Get My Will Out of a Safe Deposit Box?

If after pondering your options, you decide to leave your will in a safe deposit box, how will people get to it? The first step, as mentioned above, is making sure that the correct people know that you, in fact, have a safe deposit box and in which bank it is located. This also includes which branch of the bank it is located at.

One possibility is to share the box with someone else. Having your child as a co-signatory on your safe deposit box may be convenient for multiple reasons but will allow them to open the box and find the will easily. Of course, it also allows them to open the box with no supervision and remove items while you are alive and may not be appropriate for this reason in some circumstances.

If there is no one else who co-signed to open the box, the court can issue an order allowing a safe deposit box to be opened. This is a fairly quick and painless process as the courts understand that this is a necessary part of finding wills. The court will order the bank to open the box with you and allow you to remove the will. Other items have to stay in the box until probate has been begun.

How Do I Know If I Need to Update My Will?

A few years after getting your will done, you may start to wonder whether it needs updating. The two main reasons you might need to update your will are that your life circumstances have changed or that the law has changed.

Life circumstances changing can be the birth of a new child, divorce, death of a loved one, or any number of other things. You may have had a falling out with a friend and want a new executor. Perhaps your adult child is now the best choice for an executor, but when you signed the will, he or she was too young.

Some life circumstances, such as the birth of a new child or marriage or divorce, actually revoke the will in Georgia. If you make a will while you are single, and then get married, the court will assume that you meant to make a new will and never got around to it and revoke your will. The same is true with having a child or another child. The court will assume that you meant to leave provision for that child and revoke your will accordingly. If you get divorced and forget to change your will, the court pretends that your ex-spouse predeceased you and follows the rest of your will as it would if that person were dead. There is a way to get around this which involves specifically saying in your will that the will contemplates marriage or divorce or the birth of a new child. This should be done specifically and thoughtfully because you would not want to accidentally leave things to only two of your three children or to an ex-spouse.

The other reason you might need to update your will is if the law has changed. Periodically, when different laws come into effect, particularly related to the estate tax, the goal of estate planning can change. During some eras, it has been to pay as little estate tax as possible. In others, such as now, the goal is more about avoiding income tax. If the estate tax exclusion amount changes radically, your estate plan may well need to change radically.

While you may have to consult an attorney or keep up with the legal news to know if the law has changed, keeping up with your circumstances is up to you. I recommend taking a look at your estate planning documents once a year. Most people won't get around to it that often but should look at the documents once every five years. Make sure that everything is still correct. If there is only a small change, you may decide it's okay to leave the will as it is. However, if anything significant has changed, be sure to update your will.

Trusts

Apart from wills, trusts are the most widely known estate planning tools. What are they? Who needs one? What do I do with one if I have one?

There are three main types of trusts: a testamentary trust, a living revocable trust, and an irrevocable living trust. As previously discussed briefly when discussing wills, a testamentary trust is included in a will. A revocable trust is a standalone trust that can be changed or terminated by the grantor. An irrevocable trust cannot be terminated and has very limited options for making changes. Testamentary trusts and revocable trusts are very common, but irrevocable trusts are only used sparingly in specific circumstances.

We will discuss revocable trusts here. As a side note, irrevocable trusts should never be attempted without an attorney and for a really good reason.

A revocable trust will have a grantor and a trustee, who are often the same person. The trust, through the trustee, owns the property and is a list of instructions for what to do with that property. They are generally very lengthy and specific. There are usually alternate trustee provisions for after the grantor passes away or during the grantor's incapacity. Being both the grantor and the trustee of a revocable trust allows great control over the property.

Creating a trust does not do anything until you put property into the trust. Personal property can be placed in a trust through signing a paper assigning the personal property to the trust. It will be signed by the grantor and by the trustee accepting the property. This will not uncommonly be the same person signing in two different places. Other property which requires titles, such as cars or real property, requires that the title be changed to "_____ as trustee of the _____ trust." Bank accounts also require changing ownership.

Revocable trusts use the Social Security number of the grantor as their EIN for tax purposes. The grantor reports the trust assets on his or her tax return.

In some states, trusts are practically required. Probate can be expensive, lengthy, and difficult. Placing assets in the trust means that they don't go through probate. Luckily, Georgia does not have a difficult or expensive probate process, and the avoidance of probate is not always a managing factor when deciding whether or not have a trust.

Another attractive thing about trusts is that they are private. Probate and anything filed in the probate process is public record. Trusts are not required to be filed anywhere, and the assets in them are not displayed as public record. The exception to the non-requirement of filing is for special needs trusts which are required to be approved by the state of Georgia before implementation.

Controlling Assets Long-Term

One significant advantage of a trust over a will is that it can control assets longer. Trusts are designed to hold and manage assets and only give out certain amounts to beneficiaries at certain times and under certain circumstances. While there are legal limits to how long a trust can be in existence, the limits are very generous, and trusts can keep assets to benefit children, grandchildren, and even great-grandchildren.

In addition to the length of time that trusts can control assets, the amount of specific direction that trusts can give over the assets is also significant. For example, the trustee could be empowered to buy a grandchild a car when he or she goes to college or withhold money from a beneficiary who is using drugs. The trustee might be directed not to give money to a beneficiary who is going through a divorce so that the money cannot be a marital asset to be split in the divorce.

Trusts also sometimes just hold the money until beneficiaries reach a certain age. Often the money will not be given in one complete lump-sum but in smaller sums at certain ages until the desired age has been reached. This might look something like 10% of the trust assets at age 21, another 10% of the assets at age 25, and the remainder of the assets at age 35.

Creditor Protection for Your Beneficiaries

Another benefit of the trust is creditor protection for the beneficiaries. If the trustee of the trust is given discretion over distributions and not required to give distributions at certain times, or given the discretion to delay distributions, then creditors of the beneficiaries will have difficulty reaching the money.

Courts have decided that in a case where a trustee has discretion, beneficiaries do not have control over the assets, and creditors cannot attach them. Once the trustee has given money to the beneficiary, creditors can go after it. This structure is more difficult and less appealing to creditors.

This creditor protection only applies when someone else is the trustee with discretion. If the grantor is also the trustee, the grantor's creditors can access the trust assets for payment of debts because grantor has control over the assets. The grantor could gain creditor protection through an irrevocable trust with someone else as the trustee, but that would be a complete loss of control over your assets and is not a particularly attractive option.

Protecting Needy Beneficiaries

The trustee is often given great discretion over distributions to "needy beneficiaries." A needy beneficiary is a person who in the trustee's discretion is considered unable to manage finances in their own best interest.

Because the definition is so broad, this could be almost anyone. This could be a beneficiary with a drug or alcohol problem. It could also be the beneficiary in the middle of a divorce. This could be a beneficiary with bad financial judgment. It could be a beneficiary who is in significant debt. This does remind us of how much you need to trust anyone you appoint as trustee of a trust, but it can be a great way of preserving assets and not putting them in the hands of people might not handle them responsibly.

It is also possible for the trustee to make payments on behalf of a needy beneficiary rather than giving the money to the person. This might look like paying rent directly as opposed to giving money to the beneficiary to pay rent if there was a concern that the money might go to something other than rent.

This flexibility that is built-in to many trusts is a great tool for protecting loved ones who might act in ways not in their own best interests.

Property Outside Georgia

Even in Georgia, owning property in multiple states is a good reason to have a trust. Without a trust holding the property, probate has to be done in multiple states. If the property is in the trust, no probate needs to be done on it.

Some states are more complicated than others. Florida comes to mind. Florida is a double threat, both because probate is so difficult and expensive and because it is such a popular place for people to own property. Georgians especially, since they live so close to Florida, are prone to owning second properties there.

Placing your Florida property inside your trust prevents anyone from needing to do probate in Florida. This is also true with other states, Florida is just an example. If the property needs to be transferred/sold, the trustee of the trust is the one that will sign the deed. This is true both while the grantor is alive and after the grantor has died.

Putting your property in the trust is as easy as a new deed. This isn't terribly expensive and is a huge time and trouble saver later.

Special Types of Trusts for Special Goals

Trusts are not generic, and despite all legalese looking the same, they have very different uses and abilities. If your trust needs to serve a certain type of person or hold a certain type of property, you need to make sure that you have the right type of trust.

Often, a trust can do more than one thing, but some types of trusts are so specific that they only have one function. The next few sections give a few examples of popular types of specialty trusts.

I. IRA Trust

An IRA trust is meant to hold an IRA. This is not an item that you would want to put in a regular trust that did not include specialty provisions. The IRS has requirements for IRAs and putting them in the wrong type of trust could result in forced distributions and tax consequences.

IRAs receive quite a bit of creditor protection during the lifetime of the person who accrued them. Once the IRA goes to a beneficiary, the creditor protection is lost, and creditors of the beneficiary can get out the funds. One of the benefits of an IRA trust is that creditor protection continues for the beneficiaries.

Another benefit of an IRA trust is that it can hold funds for minors. If a regular IRA is inherited by a minor, someone will probably need to be legally appointed to manage the money. If the funds go into an IRA trust, this extra step is unnecessary.

IRAs are distributed by beneficiary designation rather than under a will. This means that to have a trust as the beneficiary, it will need to be designated in the IRA paperwork.

When the trust is drafted correctly, the IRS will look through the trust at the beneficiary and allow the beneficiary to use more advantageous distribution rules. It treats the trust as if it were not there for purposes of minimum distributions. However, if there are multiple beneficiaries of the trust, minimum distributions will be based on the oldest beneficiary. This can negatively impact younger beneficiaries and should be considered when deciding who to make a beneficiary of your IRA trust.

II. Charitable Remainder Trust

A charitable remainder trust is an irrevocable trust. The basic idea behind it is that a non-charitable beneficiary will receive income from the trust, at least yearly, for a specified period. The non-charitable recipient can be anyone you want it to be. After you pass away, the charity receives the rest of the assets.

There are tax benefits, both immediate and after death, for this type of trust. Usually, the type of asset you would want to fund a charitable remainder trust with is one that has appreciated considerably, and when sold, would normally result in a large capital gains tax. In this special kind of structure, the asset is transferred into the trust, and when the trustee sells the asset to invest in other income-producing assets, no capital gains tax is charged.

An interesting thing to note about charitable remainder trusts is that even though they are irrevocable, there is a secondary market for them. Because they are filled with income-producing assets, some companies will pay to buy the charitable remainder trust. This doesn't make it any less important to be very careful when considering a charitable remainder trust, but it is good to know if your situation has changed and a charitable remainder trust that was set up years ago is no longer working for you.

III. Special Needs Trust

A very important specialty trust is the special needs trust. This trust is designed to allow those with special needs, particularly those who need government benefits, to have some assets without knocking them out of eligibility for government benefits with asset-based eligibility standards.

Specifically, many elderly or disabled people need Medicaid. In Georgia, Medicaid has a very low threshold of assets and income that will still allow an individual to qualify for assistance. However, the number of assets that knock someone out of Medicaid eligibility is not necessarily sufficient to pay for nursing home care or other medical care that Medicaid would've provided.

A special needs trust has specific language in it that does not allow the assets to be used for room and board. It specifically states that it is not to supplant maintenance and support provided by government benefits. It can only pay for "extras" that the government benefits are not designed to pay for.

It can be disastrous when a disabled child suddenly inherits money. Much time and expense may have gone into making sure the child has qualified for Medicaid and is receiving the correct care. If the child inherits enough money to knock them out of eligibility, these services will immediately be terminated. It will be difficult and costly to figure out how to get them reinstated. Sometimes, there is nothing that can be done other than spending down the money and applying again once the financial threshold has been reached.

If a disabled person or any person on government benefits will be inheriting from you, it is important to consider making sure this inheritance comes in the form of a special needs trust.

IV. Life Insurance Trust

Another kind of trust is the life insurance trust. This type of trust is designed to own and pay for life insurance. It is also irrevocable.

The reason that you might consider a life insurance trust rather than buying and paying for life insurance personally is the increased creditor protection. This is an incredibly safe way to pass assets to beneficiaries.

The life insurance trust is responsible for paying the premium every year. Other than that, no activity takes place until after the grantor's death. Once the grantor has passed away, the life insurance is paid into the trust, and the trustee manages the assets for the beneficiaries, much like any other trust. This prevents beneficiaries with credit problems, ongoing divorces, gambling problems, or other issues from running through the life insurance proceeds irresponsibly.

Your Team

Very few people want to navigate all of these issues on their own. Having a team of advisors on your side makes the process less stressful and more likely to be done correctly.

It is important to choose knowledgeable and honest advisors. There is also no shame in shopping around to find advisors you feel comfortable with. Never settle for adding a member to your team that you don't feel 100% comfortable with.

In this day of internet reviews, be sure to run a search on the potential advisor before hiring. You may not get any information, but often you will find either positive reviews which will make you feel better about your choice or negative reviews that will keep you from making a bad choice.

Who should be on your team? Answers vary depending on what areas you already have proficiency in and what areas you need help. Good people to consider are an estate planning attorney, a financial advisor, a CPA, and a private patient advocate. (I'll also put a plug-in here for a good general practitioner doctor. Preventative healthcare and checkups may help you avoid probate for longer.)

What is a Fiduciary? (And why do I need one?)

An important thing to be aware of when choosing advisors is which of them are fiduciaries and which are not. Fiduciaries are required to give you the advice they think is best for you. They cannot consider whether the choice will make more or less money for them. Fiduciaries generally work on a fee-only structure. This means that they are being paid upfront and not receiving any secret kickbacks for selling you certain insurance products.

We certainly hope that most of the financial advisors who aren't fiduciaries are also looking out primarily for the best interest of their clients and not for the best interests of their pocketbooks. However, it is important to understand how and where someone makes their money. This helps you understand their motivation.

Estate Planning Attorney

Good news! Your estate planning attorney has fiduciary duties towards you. I thought I would go ahead and get that out of the way so you could start thinking about other things.

Attorneys have different qualifications, different levels of competence, and different amounts of knowledge. You want an attorney that specializes in estate planning. It is not uncommon for estate planning attorneys to also do business work, probate, or some other related area. This is not a problem and may even benefit you because the attorney is more likely to consider more possibilities when thinking about your situation. What you don't want is an attorney who doesn't focus on estate planning. It is true that almost any attorney can produce a will. It is also true that knowledgeable and competent attorneys who practice in other areas of the law come to estate planning attorneys to prepare their wills for them. (Really, this happens all the time.) Just being an attorney is not enough.

There are also subsections of attorneys such as those who specialize in working with small business owners, those who specialize in planning for special needs people, those who specialize in planning for especially high worth or "taxable estates," and those who specialize in planning for those who need government benefits. It is important to understand what the actual focus of an attorney's practice is to make sure you're choosing someone who regularly works with people who have the same issues you have.

Financial Planner

It is always a good idea to consult a financial planner to make sure that you are on the right track toward retirement. It may also be desirable to hire one to manage your investment assets. Few people have the energy and diligence to do the research needed to keep up with their investments.

The first thing to think about with financial planners is whether they are fiduciaries. I'm not suggesting you should refuse to work with someone who you already know and trust because they aren't a fiduciary, but it is very important to be aware of how your professionals are getting paid.

As a personal example, I once went to a financial planner who is not a fiduciary. My husband and I asked about a certain type of life insurance that had attractive features but was very expensive. It became obvious to us almost immediately that we quite literally could not afford that type of insurance, but the financial planner continued to try to push us toward it. She had a spreadsheet in front of her with a breakdown of our income and our expenses. It was just as obvious to her that this was a bad choice for us as it was to us, but she would've made a significant amount of money if she had sold us that policy. I'll personally only be working with fiduciaries from now on.

There are many different designations and institutions that confer degrees on financial planners. One I will point out to take note of is CFP. This stands for a certified financial planner, and people with this designation are in fact fiduciaries.

These are not the only people who are fiduciaries, but it's a quick and easy way to identify one.

In addition to figuring out whether someone is going to act in your best interest, you also want to know whether they know what's in your best interest. Most of the time, that means someone who has a fair amount of experience. Sometimes, that may also mean a less experienced person who has supervision within their company.

CPA

CPAs are certified, public accountants. You may want to hire one to do your taxes. Unlike financial advisors, CPAs are certified by only one institution, the American Institute of Certified Public Accountants.

While CPA is a trusted designation, they aren't fiduciaries in the regular sense of the word. Their required code of conduct, however, is very similar to the definition of fiduciary. There are also times that courts have found that CPAs were acting in a fiduciary capacity, and most CPAs do consider themselves to have a fiduciary responsibility toward their clients.

Not everyone has a complicated enough tax situation to require hiring a CPA. Many people use TurboTax or other similar do-it-yourself tax filing software with great success. However, if you become self-employed, have significant medical expenses in a year, or otherwise, have an involved financial portfolio, you may want to consider hiring CPA. The amount of relief that can come from having a professional handle your taxes is often well worth the price.

Private Patient Advocate

Lastly, I want to point out that a private patient advocate may be a good member of your team. If you or a family member are going through intense medical issues and could benefit from someone with medical knowledge, helping you deal with the hospital, insurance, and doctors you may want a private patient advocate.

I mention this profession particularly because they aren't very well known. As medical care has gotten more complicated, it has become more frustrating for the average person to deal with hospital stays that may have issues regarding inpatient or outpatient status and admission. It has also gotten more difficult at times to have the correct procedures approved by insurance.

The average person does not know what to do or even understand the problem. Sometimes all you know is that someone who is still medically fragile is about to be discharged from the hospital unreasonably soon. A private patient advocate can help look at the records and determine if there is a way to keep the patient receiving the necessary care and make sure that it is covered by insurance.

While you do have to pay out-of-pocket for this service, it is well worth it and will almost always save money in the long run.

Protecting Yourself

𝒯he next thing to discuss is protecting yourself. I've put it last because the tendency is to feel that protecting yourself is selfish. Parents particularly are always putting their children first, which is one of the things that makes them so wonderful.

However, as we will see, protecting yourself is a favor to your family and loved ones. Having a power of attorney ready for an emergency doesn't just help you, it helps them. Having an Advance Directive for Health Care completed and filed with your doctor and hospital is a favor to the person tasked with making medical decisions for you.

In many ways, I consider the Advance Directive for Health Care and power of attorney the two most important planning documents you can have. These are the documents that will be effective while you are alive and can have significant consequences.

I'm also including some discussion of digital assets in this section. This is a newer area of law because it has only been recently that email, Facebook, and other digital repositories have become so important to our lives. There continues to be a lot of friction in this area, and the laws in this area are evolving.

Power of Attorney

A power of attorney is the document that allows someone else to handle your financial and legal affairs. It authorizes your agent to do a wide variety of things such as take money out of your bank account, sell your car, sell real property, change your mailing address with the post office, and practically anything else that you would be able to do.

This is a powerful document that can be very dangerous. If the wrong person is your agent, serious financial consequences could ensue. And unfortunately, even though theft with a power of attorney is still theft, law enforcement agencies are likely to tell you this is a civil matter as soon as they hear that there is a power of attorney involved.

So why does anyone choose to have a power of attorney? Having the right person as your power of attorney can provide a lot of safety and peace of mind. If you end up in the hospital, there is someone who is already authorized to pay your bills. If you become mentally incompetent, perhaps because of Alzheimer's or dementia, there is someone able to manage your affairs.

If no power of attorney is in place when you become mentally incompetent, someone will have to go to court to become your guardian. Even if this process is started immediately, which it most likely won't be, it takes time, and a lot of damage can be done before someone has the legal authority to pay your bills, or admit you to the hospital, or move you to a new living facility.

Having a Power of Attorney is Very Important

Despite the dangers of an improperly used power of attorney, you need one. Married people often put their spouse as their first power of attorney. This can make things easier for silly things like going to the DMV about cars that are titled in both names. While this is not an overriding reason to have a power of attorney, it can be a benefit earlier than you expect.

Georgia has a new law regarding power of attorney. The law only applies to powers of attorney that have been signed after July 1, 2017. The intention of the law is to make it more difficult to misuse a power of attorney as well as make it easier to get financial institutions and third parties to accept powers of attorney.

Often banks don't want to accept powers of attorney. They have promised to keep your money safe for you and only you. A document giving someone else access to your money makes them uncomfortable and concerned about liability if it is used improperly.

The new law, with its incentives for third parties to accept properly executed powers of attorney, has a lot of people scrambling to get their powers of attorney redone. If you have an older power of attorney, it is worth considering whether you want to have a new one that falls under the authority of the new law.

An important thing to be aware of when signing a power of attorney is at the new law requires that the principal (you, the person giving authority to the agent) sign in the presence of the witness and notary with everyone present and able to see each other the entire time. This did not use to be required, but any new power of attorney signed after July 1, 2017, in Georgia which does not comply with this is completely invalid.

Name a Backup Power of Attorney

One thing I tell all my clients is to be sure to have a backup power of attorney. Naming an alternate gives you extra peace of mind. You never know when something might happen to your primary power of attorney. They could be in the car with you when you have your accident, you can no longer be married to them, or they might be unavailable because they are out of the country.

It is always easy to assume that if something happens to your initial agent, you will be able to just sign a new power of attorney. Life does not always work out this way. In our family, my husband is his grandmother's power of attorney. His father was her initial power of attorney, and my husband was the alternate. My husband's father passed away suddenly and unexpectedly. By the time he passed away, his mother was not competent to sign a new power of attorney. Because she had named her grandson as an alternate, my husband was able to step in and take care of her. He can pay her bills and deal with her doctors and her assisted living facility. Otherwise, someone would've had to go to court to become her guardian and conservator.

Having a backup is a good idea when we're talking about having an extra flashlight, but having a backup for an important document like your power of attorney is even more important.

Choosing Your Power of Attorney

Choosing someone that you trust and who is responsible and financially savvy is important. Often, the first choice will be your spouse, but this is not universally true. Sometimes, especially in blended families, the initial choice for an agent is a child. This also becomes more common with older couples who are not in good health.

If you are choosing a child or family member as your agent or as your backup agent, it is important to decide based on actual fitness for the role and not because someone is the oldest and would be hurt if a different child were chosen. If you have multiple children who are good choices, it is also worth considering whether one of them has a good relationship with all siblings and another one does not. Having someone everyone trusts will make family members less likely to quarrel.

Of course, friends are fair game as agents as well. This could be because you don't have children or other suitable family members, but it could also just be that a friend is the best choice. Not all family has an actual blood tie.

There are also professionals who can be an agent under your power of attorney. In addition to attorneys, there are so-called "daily money managers" who help seniors manage their mail and pay bills. Often, this involves a power of attorney. It is important to do your research before naming someone you don't know personally as your agent, but it is an option open to you.

Nominating a Conservator

Should you so choose, you can nominate the person acting as your agent under a power of attorney to be your conservator should you need one. The beauty of this is that you already know that you trust this person and can go ahead and tell the court, through your power of attorney, that you would want them appointed.

It is not uncommon when families are fighting to have a child who has a power of attorney from a parent and have another child that thinks that power of attorney is being abused. This often results in the second child bringing a guardianship or conservatorship action in court and asking to be appointed instead of the person that has power of attorney.

Sometimes, this is a safety feature because the agent isn't doing the right thing. However, sometimes, it is just a power struggle, and there was a reason the other child wasn't named your power of attorney. In that case, having nominated your agent for conservator will result in the court knowing what your wishes are. The court will still consider what is in your best interest for making the actual decision but will give your preferences weight.

Talking to Your Power of Attorney

Nothing defeats an excellent power of attorney document more easily than having it stored away and no one who knows to look for it. It may be incredibly well-worded, and you may have agonized over your choice of agent, but if you are unable to tell someone to go find it, it won't help you.

Most people will want to discuss the duties and responsibilities of an agent under power of attorney with their chosen agent(s). You want to make sure the person is willing to accept the responsibility. It might be that someone has too many other things going on or feels that they live too far away to do the job. It is much better to know these things now when you can do something about it rather than when it is too late.

Sometimes people feel that they would rather not tell the agent until the time comes that they are needed. The rationale is that they are safe from any possibility of financial abuse if the agent doesn't know about the appointment. This does make some logical sense and may be a route you choose to take, but the better option is not to appoint anyone as your agent that you don't trust enough to tell about the appointment.

Advance Directive for Health Care

What is an Advance Directive for Health Care? Who needs one? An Advance Directive for Health Care is a document identifying who has the authority to make medical decisions for you and giving direction to this health care agent. Anyone the age of 18 should have an Advance Directive for Health Care.

Advance Directives for Health Care are called by different things in different places. They are most commonly called living wills. This is Georgia's form of a living will.

As an adult, no one has the authority to make medical decisions for you. As soon as you turn eighteen, your parents can no longer consent to medical procedures or get medical information. While this may initially give a sense of freedom, the flip side is that if you are unable to communicate your medical choices, no one else can do it for you.

As a married adult, your spouse has a legal right to make decisions for you in the absence of an Advance Directive for Health Care, stating otherwise. Depending on your relationship with your spouse, this may make you feel more secure or cause you greater distress.

An important thing to remember while thinking about the Advance Directive for Health Care is that as long as you can advocate for yourself, the doctor will listen to you and not to your health care agent. It is only when you cannot speak for yourself, or choose not to speak for yourself, that your health care agent will be consulted.

Fill This Important Role ASAP

One of the benefits of the Advance Directive for Health Care is that there is a Georgia "statutory form." This means that the Georgia legislature has passed a law giving the form of the Advance Directive for Health Care. How does this help you? If you do a search on the internet for it, you can find a blank Advance Directive for Health Care to fill out. You may also be offered one at the hospital.

The second great thing is that while the Advance Directive for Health Care does require two witnesses, it does not require a notary. You can fill one out in the hospital if you need it or you can fill it out at home and have your next door neighbors witness it.

It is easy to fill in the blanks and get the form signed and witnessed. The catch, as usual, is that the form could stand to be a little bit easier to understand and you may want a lawyer or a medical professional to help guide you through it.

A Little Guidance

While I recommend that if you have any questions, you seek out personalized answers to your questions, here is a little guidance about the form:

Part One deals with selecting a Health Care Agent. This health care agent is the one who will be making decisions for you if you are unable to make them for yourself. This is an incredibly important thing to have in place, particularly because unmarried adults aged 18 and older do not have automatic health care agents. For parents, the moment your child turns 18, you no longer have the authority to make decisions on his or her behalf. For those who are married, your spouse has the right to make these decisions—unless you designate someone different. In the case of an estranged spouse, or one that does not share your medical treatment philosophy, it may be beneficial to nominate someone different. Additionally, people may name a secondary health care agent, just in case the primary one cannot be reached. There is a "statement of the health care agent's powers" in Part One and some options for limiting the powers, but the important part is to have someone in place in case of an emergency.

Part Two deals with treatment preferences. This gives the medical professionals guidance about your desires – even if your agent cannot be reached.

It also gives your agent confidence about making the right decisions on your behalf.

Under Part Two, Item 6 tends to confuse people. It addresses when you want your medical decisions to apply. (Selections about the use of life-saving measures comes later in the form). For Item 6, there are two places to initial, and you can initial both to make both of them apply. The first reads that Part Two will be effective if you are in "A terminal condition, which means [you] have an incurable or irreversible condition that will result in [your] death in a relatively short period." I tell people to think about this as incurable cancer. You may be delirious with pain and unable to communicate your wishes, but you are dying no matter what treatment choices the doctors make. The second option is that your choices in Part Two will be effective if you are in "A state of permanent unconsciousness, which means [you are] not aware of [yourself] or [your] environment and [you] show no behavioral response to [your] environment." For this option, I tell clients to imagine a car accident and subsequent coma. The doctors cannot wake you up and do not know if you ever will wake up, but you can continue indefinitely in your coma state. If you want your choices to apply in both situations, you will initial both places. If you only want your decisions to apply in one of the situations, you only initial that one. Most clients I deal with end up initialing both sections if they are confident in their treatment choices.

Part 2, Item 7 deals with treatment preferences and is formatted as a multiple-choice question (with one of those choices broken down even further, into sub-parts). Item 7 is the heart of the advance directive, as it provides your doctors and your health care agent with directions as to your medical wishes. "If I am in any condition that I initialed in Section (6) above and I can no longer communicate my treatment preferences after reasonable and appropriate efforts have been made to communicate with me about my treatment preferences, then:"

Choice A: "Try to extend my life as long as possible, using all medications, machines, or other medical procedures that in reasonable medical judgment could keep me alive..." Choice A is a fairly straight forward option. Select this one if you want everything possible done to save you.

Choice B: "Allow my natural death to occur. I do not want any medications, machines, or other medical procedures that in reasonable medical judgment could keep me alive but cannot cure me..." This choice does not preclude medical care that can cure your disease but won't allow anything beyond that. This option is for those who are comfortable with dying and do not want to spend a significant amount of time in hospitals, hooked up to machines. In other words, you are asking not to be put on a ventilator, or to receive nutrients/fluids if you cannot be fed by mouth. This choice does still slow for pain medication.

Choice C: "I do not want any medications, machines, or other medical procedures that in reasonable medical judgment could keep me alive but cannot cure me, except as follows..." If you initial Choice C, you are asking that your doctors only perform specific actions or procedures – beyond those treatments which may cure you. This section has four additional options. First is that you would like to receive nutrition by tube or other medical means if necessary. Second is that you want to receive fluids by tube or other medical means if necessary. Third, is that you want doctors to put you on a ventilator if you need help breathing. Fourth is that you want doctors to do cardiopulmonary resuscitation (CPR) on you if necessary. If you find yourself checking all four of these boxes, you may want to reconsider selecting Choice C, and instead choose Choice A for clarity. Otherwise, Choice C does provide more flexibility in directing doctors with specific instructions on what treatments you do want and do not want.

Part Two, Item 8, allows you to provide an additional statement, in your own words. You are not required to write anything here if you do not want to; however, it is advisable to provide additional information about your personal or religious values, as well as your personal preferences regarding pain relief. Here is an example of the language my clients have used to express their medical wishes: "I do not want my life to be prolonged nor do I want life-sustaining or death-delaying treatment to be provided or continued if my agent believes the burdens of the treatment outweigh the expected benefits. I want my agent to consider the relief of suffering, the expense involved, and the quality as well as the possible extension of my life in making decisions concerning life-sustaining or death-delaying treatment."

Part Two, Item 9 only applies to women of childbearing age. This section specifies that the individual filling out this form understands that under Georgia law, any medical choices you specify will not be carried out if you are pregnant and your fetus is viable. In that situation, doctors will make all efforts to keep you alive, to allow the fetus the best possible chance of survival. Alternatively, if you are pregnant and your fetus is not viable, Section 9 provides the option that medical choices made on your advance directive will still be carried out.

Part Three of the Georgia Advance Directive for Health Care form addresses guardianship. You can leave this part of the form blank if you want, or, you can nominate someone as your guardian if you should ever need one. Your guardian and your health care agent can be the same person – but they do not have to be. A judge has the final say on the issue of guardianship, so you will not be completely avoiding the court system, but he or she will take your written wishes into account.

Part Four is the section of the advance directive form that you sign. There is also an option to have the advance directive only effective from a certain date to another date. For most people, this is not the best option, but sometimes may be a good choice if there is a specific problem or medical procedure coming up in the near term.

Choose a Health Care Agent Who Is Comfortable With Your Treatment Choices

An important part of choosing your health care agent is choosing one whose medical treatment beliefs are similar to your own. While slight differences in approach are fine and can be overcome by trusting your agent to follow your instructions rather than their preferences, radical differences in belief can be a big problem.

If being allowed to pass with dignity and without the intervention of machines is important to you, then choosing a health care agent who does not believe in allowing someone to die for any reason would be a bad option. Choosing a family member who is suspicious of modern medicine might be a really good choice if you too have concerns about modern medicine but would be a very bad choice if you expected your agent to take the recommendations of your doctors.

Friends or relatives with medical backgrounds sometimes make great health care agents, but surprisingly, many can come with significant personal opposition to certain types of drugs, particularly pain-relieving drugs. If it is important to you to be kept as comfortable as possible no matter what, be sure your health care agent will be comfortable advocating for you to get the drugs you need.

Give Clear Instructions in Writing

Make sure your desires are spelled out in black and white for your health care agent. This makes difficult decisions easier because the agent can be confident in following your wishes.

Sometimes health care agents are called on to do very hard things. Deciding to take someone off of a ventilator or deciding not to have one used in the first place, is an incredibly difficult and emotional choice. Even when your agent has clear instructions that you do not want to be on a ventilator, being put in the position of making the actual choice is difficult. Add to this the possibility that other family members may disagree with your decisions and disagree with your health care agent for honoring your decisions, and there is some serious possibility for family conflict.

The kindest thing you can do is to put your choices down clearly in black and white. While your family may disagree with your wishes, at least you can make sure that no one ever has to second guess what you wanted.

Nominating a Guardian

The Advance Directive for Health Care form gives you the option of nominating a guardian in Part Three of the form. This is an optional section and can be left blank if you don't want to nominate a guardian.

The options are to nominate the person currently serving as your health care agent or to nominate a specific person whose information you write it. The nomination only takes effect if you should become in need of a guardian. As long as you are healthy and of sound mind, nothing happens.

If you do need a guardian, the nomination in the Advance Directive for Health Care is not the same as a legal guardianship. A judge will still have to appoint a guardian for you. However, the Advance Directive for Health Care can be used as evidence by the person asking to be appointed as your guardian. This will show the judge who you wanted your guardian to be.

Sometimes, it isn't a big deal because there is only one logical guardian or there are several possible guardians and all of them are good. Other times it can be very important to make your wishes known.

Talking to Your Health Care Agent

Although it is important to give clear written instructions to your health care agent, it is also valuable to sit down and talk to your health care agent. Discussing your thoughts on medical care and what types of medical care you would like or would not like will help your health care agent make decisions confidently for you.

One way to approach this conversation is by thinking about healthcare situations you've been involved in either directly or on the periphery of and think about what went wrong or what went right. It can be easier to describe why you want a specific treatment or would never want treatment if you are telling a story and can explain to your health care agent what happened in the past and how it affected you or the family members of the ill person.

Another important thing to remember while having this conversation is that you are empowering your health care agent to make decisions for you just as you would make for yourself. It isn't a sad time because we need to dwell on the possibilities of everything that can go wrong, it is a way of being confident that no matter what the circumstances your wishes will be carried out. Approaching the conversation in the right frame of mind can have a big impact on whether it is a relatively pleasant conversation or difficult one for both you and your health care agent.

During the conversation, you must stop and listen to your health care agent. He or she may have questions to ask, but also express thoughts on medical treatment. If you find that the thoughts that are expressed are too far from your own or do not align with your values, and you may want to choose a different health care agent. This is true even if the person you are talking to you is expressing a willingness to abide by your decisions. In the heat of the moment, they are more likely to make different decisions than you want if there is an internal conflict between their natural tendencies and your desires.

HIPAA Authorization

Another important document to have available for your health care agent is a HIPAA authorization. "HIPAA" stands for Health Insurance Portability and Accountability Act of 1996 and is the law that regulates the privacy of medical records.

Without a HIPAA compliant authorization, another person cannot get your medical records. While it is certainly true that the doctor in the hospital is going to talk to your agent, there may be a need to get physical copies of medical records from another doctor's office. If you call the doctor's office and ask for copies of medical records, the office will tell you they need a HIPAA authorization. You will not be able to get the medical records that you are requesting without one.

The Advance Directive for Health Care contains language stating that the agent is authorized to access HIPAA-protected medical records. However, doctor's offices may be reluctant to accept this since it doesn't follow their normal procedures. Doctor's offices and hospitals have their HIPAA forms, which they would prefer to be filled out and signed, however, it may not be possible or convenient to get one filled out at the moment. The patient may not be able to sign one. Having had authorization already signed can make things much easier.

Physician Orders for Life-Sustaining Treatment (POLST)

I will only touch briefly on physician orders for a life-sustaining treatment known as POLST for short. Mostly, this is because attorneys don't have anything to do with these. A medical doctor must sign a POLST.

The form is used to get information about your treatment preferences such as whether you want to be resuscitated, whether you want feeding tubes, or whether you want certain types of drugs. The legislative act that brought the POLST into creation gives immunity to persons who act per the directives given in the POLST. This means that if someone is not resuscitated because that was what was in the POLST, there can be no lawsuit against care providers. This sometimes has caused a problem because healthcare providers err on the side of caution and resuscitate individuals who didn't wish to receive such treatment. If it is very important to you not to receive such treatment, having this in place will make it more likely that your wishes are obeyed.

The law intends for these POLSTs to be available to those who are expected to pass away within the next 365 days or who have been diagnosed with a degenerative disease such as dementia. If the form has been signed by the patient and the doctor, all instructions are to be carried out. If the patient has the capacity and chooses not to sign one, no one else can sign one on their behalf. However, if a patient does not have the capacity to sign, an authorized person may sign one on their behalf. There is a list of people authorized to sign, but the health care agent is at the top of the list. There are certain differences, such as required doctor signatures for DNR orders, if the person signing is not the health care agent.

You may want to discuss physician orders for life-sustaining treatment with your doctor if this sounds like something you would like. The form is available online but should be used as part of a treatment discussion between you and your doctor.

Digital Assets

What are digital assets, and why do I care what happens to them? At a base level, they are items stored electronically in a binary format that involve rights of some kind. These rights could be an actual ownership interest, or they could be a license to use. Although new things are being invented constantly, this definition would currently include emails, computer files, digital documents, audio and video content stored online, files stored on tablets and Kindles, social media profiles, YouTube videos, telecommunication devices, electronic storage devices such as external hard drives, and anything else that is connected to the internet.

Once you start thinking about it, you probably have a fair number of digital assets. I have quite the voluminous Kindle library, not to mention lots of pictures on Facebook and emails going back for years.

What happens to this stuff when you pass away? Who has access to your email or Facebook account? The question may not sound all that interesting until you start to imagine someone else browsing through your emails or private Facebook messages. Maybe even imagine your parents reading things that were never intended for them.

It is important to make sure your estate planning documents properly address how you want digital assets handled and who you want to do the handling.

During Life: Should Your Power of Attorney Have Access to Your Digital Assets?

Before we even start thinking about what happens to your digital assets after you die, there are some interesting questions about dealing with your digital assets while you're still alive. The first question is whether you want your power of attorney to have access to your digital assets.

If you are in the hospital, would you want your power of attorney to be able to go online and pay bills, monitor your email for important documents, or maybe let social media friends know what was going on? Now that so many bills only come by email, if your power of attorney does not have access to your email, there could be quite a few bills that are going unpaid. Having access to email makes it more likely that nothing will slip through the cracks.

On the other hand, just because you are in the hospital, does that mean you want someone browsing through your email? Do you want someone to have access to your private messages on Facebook or LinkedIn? It is entirely possible for someone who logged in to an email account for a legitimate reason to end up seeing things you don't want them to.

There is no right or wrong answer for whether you want your power of attorney to have access to your digital assets. As digital assets become more enmeshed in our lives, it will become both more difficult to keep them out and more intrusive to have them in. The key is to decide what you prefer.

If you would feel worse worrying the bills were being missed, then give your power of attorney access. If you would feel worse wondering if someone was browsing your private email, don't give them access.

An interesting thing to consider is having a separate power of attorney for digital assets. It is entirely possible that you might have a friend or sibling who you would feel more comfortable logging into your email or Facebook then you would your parents. There's absolutely nothing to prevent having a separate person as your digital asset power of attorney.

During Life: Designations with Social Media

Another thing to keep in mind is that social media is evolving and often allowing users to designate others who should have access to their accounts. This area is rapidly changing, and I won't attempt to list options or how to access them because by the time you go to look for them the name will have changed or the way of accessing will have changed.

The important thing is that if you have a social media account that you care about, you find out what settings they have. This is particularly good because it gets around the problem of user contracts between you and the company. Sometimes even when someone has a valid power of attorney, the user agreement does not allow third-parties access. While legislation is being passed in some states in this area, and Georgia may very well follow suit in the near future, right now the user agreements is the ultimate authority.

After Death: Who Should Have Access?

After your death, do you want your executor to have access to your digital assets? Unquestionably, having access will make things much easier. As mentioned previously, bills are often sent via email. Your bank statements are probably also there as well as investment account statements. It will make things incredibly much easier for your executor to have access to your email.

But do you want someone to have the ability to browse through every email you have ever sent? There are certain pictures you want your family to have, but do you want them to have access to every picture? Particularly if you've ever sent anything slightly risqué, the idea of a family member having access to this may be appalling.

Unless people have strong feelings against letting their executor have access to their digital assets, I recommend specifically mentioning digital assets in their will. This makes things easier and allows for precious photos and other mementos to be saved more easily.

Sometimes though, the person who should be in charge of the rest of your state is not the same as the person you want in charge of your digital assets. You can formally appoint someone different to be in charge of your digital assets. You can also informally have a friend or close relative in charge of cleaning things up for you. It might feel better to have a friend have access to your accounts. The friend would be able to save anything important and make sure that your executor got it, but would make sure that private matters were kept private.

After Death: Memorial Accounts on Social Media

Another option that is becoming more popular on social media accounts is a memorial setting. Facebook allows for memorial accounts, and others are following suit. For some people having this account feels less traumatic than deleting a loved one completely. For others, the idea of an account dedicated to a deceased person feels creepy.

On some level, this may be a choice that you want to discuss with your loved ones because they will be the ones who may wish you to have a memorial account. However, you should also think about whether you would want such a thing.

Each social media platform has its own rules and its settings. You will want to investigate the options for any site that you are an active participant on.

Implementing Your Estate Plan

*N*ow that you've thought through the issues and made your estate choices, the only thing left to do is to implement your estate plan. The first step is deciding whether you want to do it yourself or hire an attorney. You want to pay special attention to beneficiary designations and make sure your property is titled so that it will pass in the way you mean for it to pass.

If you are using an attorney, you will want to find one that is a good fit you and is knowledgeable of estate law. This will involve looking for recommendations and doing some research.

The important part is that you do take action.

Do It Yourself or Use An Attorney?

There are quite a few do-it-yourself options for wills and powers of attorney. The internet is full of them. The internet is also full of attorneys advertising their services.

I cannot promote any specific do-it-yourself option, but I will say that many of them if used correctly, work well. The important thing is to make you understand what you are doing and ensure that the documents are signed and witnessed properly. If done incorrectly, which is much more likely to happen with do-it-yourself options, your will may not be valid, and the choices you thought you were making won't play out as you'd hoped.

I think the wisest choice for most people is consulting a knowledgeable attorney who understands the law and can help you ensure everything is in order and properly executed. If you are going to go to all the trouble of making choices, make sure they stick.

I hope this book has given you new information to make you feel confident in your skills to do your estate plan yourself. You may also not be in a financial position to consult the services of an attorney. If that is the case, I hope you feel empowered to move forward without one using this guide to help you protect your family, your assets, and yourself.

Beneficiary Designations

When implementing your estate plan, remember to pay special attention to beneficiary designations. If the designations are wrong, your entire plan can go haywire.

Unlike old wills, which are invalidated by divorce, beneficiary designations stay in full force and effect. If you forget to change the designation, your ex-spouse could easily inherit from you.

By the same token, items subject to beneficiary designations do not pass under your will. If the beneficiary designation states that person A receives the money and your will says that person B receives the money, the beneficiary designation prevails, and person A receives it.

Additionally, keep in mind that minors may not be a good choice to inherit directly. This can create a lot of issues — you may want your estate or trust as the beneficiary. However, tax and distribution issues differ with each of these choices, and you need to make sure you are aware of the implications of the choices you make.

Even if you think you remember what your designation was, it is best practice to go back and check the paperwork to refresh your memory. If you find that you don't have a copy of your designation form handy, ask the company for a copy. Better to shuffle a little paperwork than to end up with an unintended outcome.

Property Titling

Another important thing to double-check is the titling on any real property. There can be serious consequences to having a piece of property as tenants in common rather than as joint tenants with right of survivorship.

Specifically, joint tenants with right of survivorship give the surviving owner full ownership of the property automatically. If a husband and wife own property as tenants in common and have children, if either the husband or wife dies and there is no will, the remaining spouse owns the property partially with children. Because of this potential issue, it is a best practice to check and recheck the property titling and to include real property in your will even if you know that it will pass your spouse by operation of law. There is no harm in listing it twice.

Choosing an Attorney

If you decide to get help with your estate plan, choose your attorney carefully. It is always a good idea to ask for recommendations from friends or family, but don't forget to do your due diligence online as well.

There are many sites where you can find attorney reviews. It is always a good idea to search the attorney's name and see what pops up. Some attorneys won't show up at all, particularly those without a strong internet presence, but this is a quick and easy way to come up with information.

Also check out the State Bar website, www.gabar. org, to make sure that the lawyer is an active member of the bar and has not received discipline.

Don't forget to check out the attorney's website and any other online presence. This can give you a lot of information about the attorney and give you a good idea of how knowledgeable and experienced they are.

Lastly, have a meeting with an attorney and see how you feel about them in person. Even if you have paid a consultation fee, do not be afraid to walk away if you find the attorney isn't the right fit for you. If you are not comfortable with the attorney's personality or knowledge, it is better to lose a few hundred dollars than to find later that your fears were justified after the attorney does a poor job. Alternately, if you meet the right attorney on the first try, don't feel that you must go out and get the standard three quotes. If you found the right one, there's no point in wasting your time visiting others.

Conclusion

Now, it's time to put your new knowledge into action.

If the idea of creating an estate plan seems overwhelming, I suggest breaking it down into steps such as asking friends for suggestions of attorneys, researching attorneys online, and then calling an attorney's office. Put these steps on your calendar at a time when you will be able to complete them. It doesn't matter if there is some time between step one and step two, as long as you're moving in the right direction.

Good luck and let me know if there's any way I can help you!

About the Author

Sarah Siedentopf is an estate planning and probate attorney who helps individuals and families with wills, trusts, probate, and end of life planning. Her firm, Siedentopf Law, is conveniently located in the Buckhead/Brookhaven area of Atlanta, Georgia. Sarah is particularly passionate about helping clients navigate complicated, emotional issues and making the process as easy and stress-free as possible. Sarah has earned a number of awards and honors in her legal career, including most recently the Super Lawyer's Rising Star in Estate Law (2020, 2019), Daily Report's Best Social Mediator (2019), Atlanta Legal Aid Pro Bono Star (2018), Thompson Reuter's Lead Counsel Rating in Estate Planning (2018), and Atlanta Attorney at Law Magazine's Attorney to Watch (2018, 2017).

Licensed to practice law in both Georgia and Tennessee, Sarah earned her law degree from the University Of Tennessee College Of Law and practiced in northern Virginia before opening her own estate planning law firm in Atlanta — Siedentopf Law. To learn more about her practice, visit her website www.EstateLawAtlanta.com.

Sarah is actively engaged with the local bar and

continuing education. She is a past chair of the Atlanta Bar Association Elder Law Section, a former board member, and still actively involved with the Women in the Profession Section. She is also a member of the Estate Planning and Probate Section and serves on its journal, The Mortmain. Sarah also volunteers with the Atlanta Legal Aid Society and the DeKalb Volunteer Lawyers Foundation.

When Sarah is not helping her clients or volunteering within the Atlanta legal community, she enjoys cracking open a good book, spending time with her dog, and challenging her husband to a board game.

Made in the USA
Columbia, SC
27 January 2022

54871103R00059